THE
PYRAMIDS

THE PYRAMIDS

CHARTWELL
BOOKS, INC.

Published by Chartwell Books
A Division of Book Sales Inc.
114 Northfield Avenue
Edison, New Jersey 08837
USA

Copyright ©1998 Quantum Books Ltd

0-7858-1000-5

This book is produced by
Quantum Books Ltd
6 Blundell Street
London N7 9BH

Project Manager: Rebecca Kingsley
Project Editor: Judith Millidge
Designer: Wayne Humphries
Editor: Sarah Halliwell

The material in this publication previously appeared in
Egyptology, *Pyramids* & *Ancient Egyptians*

QUMPYP
Set in Times
Reproduced in Singapore by United Graphic Ltd
Printed in Singapore by Star Standard Industries (Pte) Ltd

CONTENTS

INTRODUCTION

Many of the world's largest modern buildings are tall and rectangular, like skyscrapers, or have enormous domes, such as St. Peter's church in Rome. But builders in ancient times used a completely different shape, known as the pyramid. These buildings have four triangular sides which slope inward to a point, or a small, flat top where a temple might be built.

From the golden desert sands, Egypt's pyramids soar into the air, proclaiming the power and majesty of the god-kings – the pharaohs – who built them. The pyramids served as magnificent royal tombs: within their stone walls, secret passages led to a chamber in which the casket of the pharaoh was placed.

Above: The pyramids of Giza (c. 2500 B.C.).

Since the Ancient Egyptians believed in life after death, they buried the pharaohs together with a variety of objects for use in the next world, ranging from elaborate jewelry to wooden boats. It was the presence of treasures such as these that attracted robbers who, despite ingenious devices to deter them, almost always succeeded in entering and ransacking the tombs.

The most famous pyramids are found in Egypt, and were built as tombs for the pharaohs. Some are more than 4500 years old. The first pyramid ever built was the step pyramid at Saqqara. And the greatest are the three that rise up from the desert near the Egyptian capital of Cairo. Of these, the largest is the Great Pyramid of King Khufu. The volume of this amazing structure is so vast that five huge cathedrals could be enclosed within its walls.

No one knows why the pyramid's triangular shape was chosen in the first place. It is possible that ancient peoples regarded it as holy because it pointed toward the heavens. The pyramids may even have been built to resemble mountains, where the ancient gods lived. If this is the case, it is not surprising that temples were built on the tops of pyramids. This would have made the worshipers feel that they were closer to their gods. The Egyptians appear to have seen pyramids as staircases on which their dead kings could climb up to heaven.

Many different civilizations adopted the pyramid shape in their building, but for different ends. The Aztec civilization, for example, used their pyramids as places of sacrifice to the gods, while the Teotihuacan pyramid in Mexico was an important religious center.

Although the great age of pyramid-building ended in ancient times, the pyramid still survives in the modern world. Perhaps the most spectacular example is the glass pyramid built at the Louvre Museum in Paris, France.

Right: Aerial view of the middle pyramid of King Khafra – at the apex is the remains of the original fine stone casing.

THE
BEGINNINGS

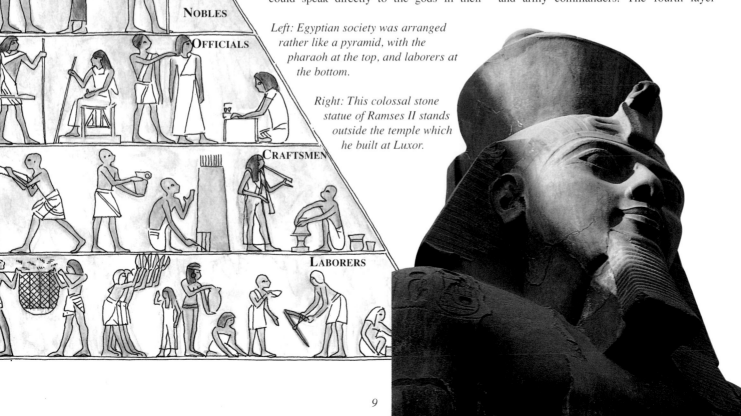

T he most famous pyramids in the world were built by the Ancient Egyptians. Some are 4500 years old. Egypt's pyramids served as immense royal tombs in which the casket of the most important member of society was placed – the pharaoh. Many people are unaware that any other pyramids exist beside the three immense examples at Giza. There are, in fact, remains of about 80 pyramids in Egypt, while there are more than 100 later, less substantial, ones in the Sudan.

A TOMB FOR THE PHARAOH

To the Egyptians, their pharaoh was much more than just a king. He was the living image of a god, come down to Earth. As such, he was respected, feared and, occasionally, worshiped. The pharaoh was the only person who could speak directly to the gods in their temples. He gave them gifts of food and wine and, in return, asked them to send blessings to the people he ruled. Egyptian society was arranged rather like a pyramid. The pharaoh was at the top. Then came high priests and nobles. Lower down were priests, officials, and army commanders. The fourth layer

Left: Egyptian society was arranged rather like a pyramid, with the pharaoh at the top, and laborers at the bottom.

Right: This colossal stone statue of Ramses II stands outside the temple which he built at Luxor.

PHARAOH

NOBLES

OFFICIALS

CRAFTSMEN

LABORERS

included skilled craftsmen. And at the bottom came laborers and peasants.

AN IMPORTANT ROLE

An Egyptian pharaoh had many roles to fulfill. As well as having religious duties, he was responsible for running the government. He had to maintain law and order, protect temples and lead his armies to war. A pharaoh had to be good at managing people. He needed to win the support of powerful nobles and chief priests, to stop them plotting against him.

A pharaoh also had to make sure that his government officials used their power to benefit the country, not just to make money for themselves. He received foreign ambassadors in his palace, and made peace treaties with kings and princes from distant lands. Often, this meant marrying a foreign princess to strengthen the alliance. Some pharaohs had a great many "official" wives.

LIFE AFTER DEATH

Many people are under the false impression that the pyramids were built by slaves for a tyrannical pharaoh. It is unlikely that the Egyptians had any slaves at this time, as their society was largely composed of peasant farmers. For three months of every year, during the inundation season, the men were unable to work in the fields, and would therefore be idle anyway.

The concerted efforts of these peasant farmers to build their pharaoh's tomb was justified by their belief that he was a god. The pharaoh was thought to be the son of the sun,

Right: Ramses wearing the most elaborate kind of royal crown.

Above: The step pyramid of King Djoser at Saqqara, built around 2650 B.C.

who had taken human form to lead the people whom he would continue to assist in the next world.

The Ancient Egyptians believed in life after death, and so, because their pharaoh was so important to them, they prepared him or her for the afterlife with immense care. They believed that by carefully preserving a dead body they would also preserve its spirit and give it everlasting life. A tomb was, therefore, a "house of eternity." As a result, the pharaohs were buried with a variety of objects for use in the next world, ranging from elaborate jewelry to wooden boats.

Pharaohs usually planned their own tomb while they were still alive, and aimed to surround themselves not only with great treasures and luxuries, but also with mundane, everyday objects that they would need in the next life. This selection could include their favorite workmen, most loyal servants, and most treasured pets. The pyramid was a place to store the casket and keep these possessions safe – although this did not always happen.

It is not certain why the Egyptians favored the pyramid form. According to Egyptian texts, the pyramid may have been seen as a staircase, or a "ramp of sunlight," on which the deceased

Above: A fine early ivory standing figure of a king discovered at Abydos, probably dating from the first dynasty, c. 3000 B.C. The pharaoh wears the white crown of upper Egypt.

pharaoh could ascend to heaven. The sun played a central part in religious beliefs throughout Egyptian history: the sun god Ra became important as early as the second dynasty (*c.* 2700 B.C.) and almost certainly had some connection with the building of the pyramids. By the fifth dynasty (*c.* 2400 B.C.), Ra had become the supreme state god who was closely associated with the pharaoh. The king took the title "son of Ra," and it was believed that after death he also joined his father Ra in heaven.

THE FIRST PYRAMIDS

The Egyptians began to built the first true pyramids in about 2600 B.C. Before then, they buried their dead in the dry sand or later in a type of tomb known as a mastaba. This was a low, rectangular structure covering an underground burial chamber. Until the third dynasty, the traditional form of royal tomb was a mastaba. These were mainly large rectangular, flat-topped buildings with sloping sides. Beneath were the burial chambers and rooms cut deep into the bedrock. Usually built in mud-brick, they were like architectural forms of prehistoric burial mounds. The earliest surviving pyramid, the famous step pyramid at Saqqara, was itself originally conceived as a mastaba. At some stage the plans were altered, and the pyramid grew into a series of six progressively diminishing terraces. Mastaba tombs later developed into the step pyramid.

THE STEP PYRAMID

The step pyramid at Saqqara is the oldest large stone building in the world, and the earliest pyramid constructed in Egypt. Saqqara, which lies in the desert west of the Nile, was the necropolis, or cemetery, of Memphis, the ancient capital of Egypt. The step pyramid dominates the area. This extraordinary monument was built in about 2650 B.C. by Pharaoh Djoser, who reigned from 2668 to 2649 B.C.

Djoser's architect was Imhotep, who was also the king's vizier, or prime minister. Imhotep's great achievement led him to be revered by later generations as a god of wisdom. He was worshiped not only as an architect but also as a doctor, magician, astronomer, and mathematician. In later times, the Greeks even identified him with Asclepius, their god of healing. But he is best remembered for designing the step pyramid.

Imhotep began the pyramid as a mastaba tomb. By adding other mastabas on top of the first, he created a stepped structure with six vertical stages: a step pyramid. Beneath the pyramid, archeologists found a maze of passages and rooms. Djoser's burial chamber was lined with pink granite and sealed with a stone that weighed three tons. But it was plundered by thieves long ago, and only the king's mummified left foot was found inside.

FUNERARY ARCHITECTURE

The step pyramid is the major feature in a vast complex of funerary architecture. These buildings and courtyards acted as a kind of stage set for the dead king to perform his funerary rites. They are of great importance because, being made of stone, they have survived, when most earlier mud-brick structures have disintegrated. The step pyramid it-

Far left: The step pyramid adjacent to a mastaba tomb, from which its structure developed.

Below: The step pyramid at Saqqara is the first pyramid ever built. Early Egyptian pyramids consisted of several steps, as here.

Above: After 30 years of his reign, Pharaoh Djoser would have been recrowned king of Egypt at a special festival - the herb-seed festival – that took place at the Saqqara pyramid. Here, he wears the crown of upper and lower Egypt.

Right: Bronze statuette of Imhotep, the architect of the earliest step pyramid at Saqqara. In later times, Imhotep was worshiped as a god of wisdom. (c. 600 B.C.) (British Museum.)

Left: The pyramid at Maidum represents the transitional stage of development from the step pyramid to the "true" pyramid. It was originally conceived as a step pyramid and subsequently modified to a true pyramid by means of additional casing, but the enormous pressures thus created led to its partial collapse.

self stands at the center of a walled site, with a series of courtyards around it. The outer walls extended 1790 feet (545 meters) from north to south, and 910 feet (277 meters) from east to west. There were 14 doorways in the walls; 13 of them were false.

AN IMPRESSIVE SIGHT
In its day, the sight of this wall of shining white limestone, with the pyramid rising out of it, must have been a majestic spectacle. Standing on the edge of a plateau overlooking the ancient capital of Memphis, it must have represented a great symbol of the eternal power of their god-king to the Egyptians who built it. Its clean, sharp edges have since been blurred through the passage of time, and its finely worked limestone casing has been plundered, yet it is still impressive, rising to a height of 200 feet (60 meters).

The body of King Djoser was never found and, like most tombs, the pyramid had been looted in ancient times. However, two alabaster sarcophagi were discovered, one containing the body of a child, while some 30,000 stone vases were also found in the precinct.

FROM STEP TO "TRUE"
The pyramid underwent several stages of development during the next century before the great Giza pyramids. How the step pyramid developed into a "true" pyramid – that is, one with smooth sides – can by seen in the pyramids at Maidum and Dahshur.

The Maidum pyramid was probably started by King Huni and completed by his successor, King Sneferu (2613-2589 B.C.). It seems originally to have been stepped, then modified to become straight-sided. At some time in antiquity, the pyramid's outer layers of masonry collapsed, leaving merely a mound of sand and rubble, and exposing the pyramid's inner, tower-like core – the curious structure which survives today. This inner core is now the only part of the pyramid to exist, revealing the remains of the steps beneath. A passageway, which was never fully completed, descended through the mass of the pyramid to the burial chamber. The pyramid was built as an eight-tiered structure whose steps were filled in with local stone to make it a true pyramid. The whole building was then covered with a "skin" of fine limestone. Why and when the outer layers collapsed is still a mystery.

REALISTIC STATUES

Several miles south of Saqqara, at Dahshur, King Sneferu built the so-called "bent" pyramid, which is not stepped but straight-sided, except for a curious change of angle in the middle. This is because architects, fearing it would collapse, reduced the angle halfway up and created a pyramid with a unique, "bent" shape. It is clear from this pyramid that Egyptian architects at this time were still wondering how steep the sides of a pyramid could be before they became unstable. Also known as the "Gleaming Pyramid of the South," it paved the way for the greatest of the true pyramids – the pyramids at Giza. Sneferu's son and successor was probably Khufu, and he selected the imposing site at Giza to build the most perfect, impressive pyramid of all.

Right: Statues of Rahotep, Sneferu's son, and Nofret, Rahotep's wife, found in a tomb near the Maidum pyramid. Their eyes are made from volcanic glass, making them look incredibly realistic. When people saw them for the first time, they were frightened.

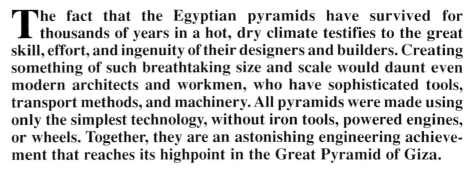

The fact that the Egyptian pyramids have survived for thousands of years in a hot, dry climate testifies to the great skill, effort, and ingenuity of their designers and builders. Creating something of such breathtaking size and scale would daunt even modern architects and workmen, who have sophisticated tools, transport methods, and machinery. All pyramids were made using only the simplest technology, without iron tools, powered engines, or wheels. Together, they are an astonishing engineering achievement that reaches its highpoint in the Great Pyramid of Giza.

Quarrying Stone

The supply of so much stone demanded intensive quarrying, and the large demand would have required specialist quarrymen. The Ancient Egyptians possessed little more than primitive copper chisels, so they must have developed a specialized technique for extracting the stone. It was easier to cut the softer limestone than the hard granite. The poorer quality limestone was extracted quite easily, by open-case quarrying, since it lay on the surface. However, tunneling was required to obtain the finer Tura limestone and the granite. This was probably assisted by the application of heat and water. Wooden wedges were driven into cracks in the stone, then soaked in water, causing them to expand and separate the stone. The blocks were squared up using chisels and mallets.

Copper saws were also used, perhaps with jewel chippings to assist the cutting. In order to work the granite, they had to pound it with balls of an even harder stone called dolerite. Although the majority of limestone blocks which formed the core were only roughly finished, the facing stones had to be cut with great precision.

Most of these have since been looted by the stonemasons of Cairo, but those which remain at the base, where sand covered them, fit so closely that the joints are almost invisible. They would have been smoothed off after they were put in place when the building of the pyramid was completed. Enormous waste dumps of limestone chippings from working the blocks have been discovered nearby. It

Left: Close-up view of Khufu's Great Pyramid, showing the massive stone blocks, carefully fitted together.

HOW WERE PYRAI BUILT?

Below: Wooden wedges were inserted and soaked in water to make them swell, which shattered the stone so that it could be removed.
Bottom: Strong wooden poles were used to lever out the stone blocks.
Right: The huge blocks of stone used to build the pyramids were very heavy. Many workers must have been crushed to death in the quarry mines.

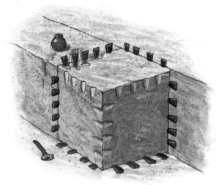

PYRAMID CONSTRUCTION

Clockwise from right: Internal construction: most true pyramids are formed from a series of buttress walls with masonry coatings, built around a central core.

There are many theories concerning the placement of building ramps. Assuming the step pyramid within the pyramid was built first, the ramps could have run from one step to the next rather than approaching the pyramid face at right angles.

Center: Building ramps: the pyramid builders were faced with the problem of how to lift the heavy stone blocks to the required height. The only method proved to have been used by the Ancient Egyptians is based on ramps.

Geometrical precision: the slightest error in the angle of incline of a pyramid would have resulted in a substantial misalignment of the edges at the apex.

Bottom: Some of the pyramid measurements show an accurate use of mathematical formulae. The mathematical knowledge of the Egyptians would not have been advanced enough to arrive at this calculation, but it could have been produced "accidentally'," for example, through measuring distances by counting revolutions of a drum.

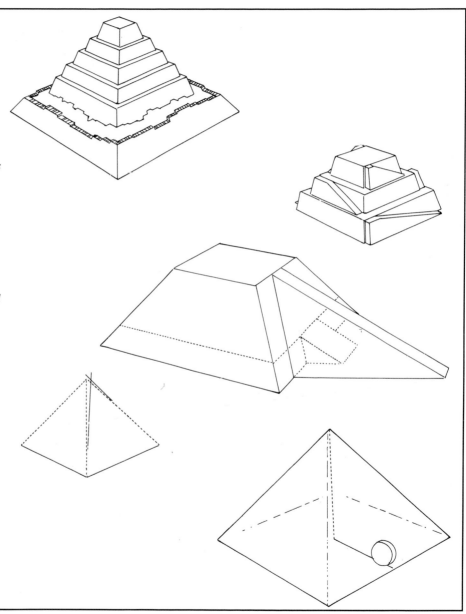

has been estimated that the stone from these dumps is of an equivalent volume to over half that of the pyramids.

CONSTRUCTING THE PYRAMIDS

Pyramids were built in several stages. The foundations were leveled, and base stones laid. Then sloping ramps were built out of rubble. Heavy stone blocks were dragged up these ramps as the "steps" of the pyramid were built. Smaller blocks were used to form a

Below: The workmen's village at Deir-el-Medina.

smoothly sloping shape. The blocks of stone used to build the pyramids are enormous. On average, they are as big as, and weigh more than, a family car. It was a tremendous achievement to transport them and lift them into place.

The problem of how to lift the heavy stone to the required height was a testing one. The only method proved to have been used by the ancient Egyptians is based on ramps. These were built of mud-brick and rubble, and sledges were used to drag the blocks up – wheeled transport was not used in the pyramid age.

As the pyramid grew higher, the length of the ramp and the width of its base were increased to prevent it from collapsing. Several ramps approaching the pyramid from different sides were probably used. There are many theories concerning the placement of building ramps. Assuming the step pyramid within the pyramid was built first, the ramps could have run from one step to the next rather than approaching the pyramid at right angles.

As for internal construction, most true pyramids are formed from a series of buttress walls with masonry coatings, built around a central core. The height of the buttress walls decreases from the center outward, thus forming a step structure which adds stability to the structure. Packing blocks were used to fill the "steps," and casing blocks completed the transformation into a true pyramid.

THE WORKERS

Peasant farmers carried out the purely physical labor, but there must have been many skilled workers engaged in this vast building project. They worked in gangs and many stones have their names still painted on them, such as "Boat Gang," "South Gang," and "Enduring Gang." The stone would still have to be worked into blocks and finished by stonemasons. Men with building skills would then be needed to lay the blocks level and close together. The majority of the workforce was involved in moving the stone only when they could not work the fields, but these more

Left: Statues carved in the rock face at the tomb of Quar, at Giza, not far from the Great Pyamid. Many officials and priests were buried here, to be near the pharaohs.

specialist workers would be employed permanently on the pyramid or in the quarries. Near the Great Pyramid, barracks or lodgings for 4000 men have been excavated. From the tools discovered there, it is likely that they were occupied as builders and stonemasons working on the pyramids. The laborers were mostly villagers, conscripted by the pharaoh's officials, in the same way that other men were sent to join the army. They were paid their wages in food – bread, dried meat, and beer – and lived in specially-built villages set up around the construction site.

THE GREAT PYRAMID

The superior construction, scale, and accessibility to Cairo of the Giza pyramids have made them the most famous of all the pyramids still standing. The three pyramids of Giza are the largest and most impressive monuments to have survived from antiquity, and are the only one of seven wonders of the ancient world still surviving. Built by the pharaohs of the fourth dynasty, from 2613–2498 B.C., the pyramids of Giza were as ancient to the Romans as the Romans are to us. The biggest and oldest of the three is the most immense stone monument ever built on Earth. Known as the Great Pyramid, it was made as a tomb for Pharaoh Khufu (2589-2566 B.C.). To the right of the Great Pyramid lies the pyramid of Khafre, Khufu's son, while to the left of it stands the smallest of the three, the pyramid of Menkaure, Khafre's son.

ROYAL TOMBS

Despite many fanciful theories, these pyramids were simply tombs of the pharaohs. They all contained sarcophagi, or caskets, and are situated on the west bank of the Nile, where the Egyptians traditionally buried their dead. Like all pyramids, they were built in groups and were part of a vast cemetery complex. This included mortuary temples and tombs of other members of the royal family and court, as well as numerous priests and officials.

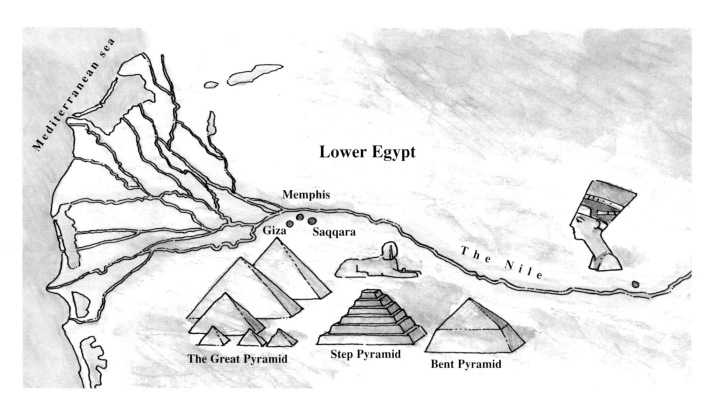

Lower Egypt

Memphis

Giza   Saqqara

The Nile

The Great Pyramid   **Step Pyramid**   **Bent Pyramid**

Above: The River Nile provided a long strip of fertile land, perfect for growing crops. Including the Delta, it covered about 21,000 square miles (34,000 square kilometers).

Right: The kingdom of Ancient Egypt grew up along the banks of the River Nile in North Africa. It was well-positioned for contact with both Mediterranean and Middle Eastern early civilizations.

KHUFU

KHAFRE

MENKAURE

Above: The three pharaohs who built the Giza pyramids are pictured here beside their "cartouches."'

Although the Giza pyramids are unique, their perfect form developed from much earlier royal tomb structures.

The Great Pyramid could only have been built by a king who exercised complete control over the economic resources of the country. The large quantities of stone, the unlimited manpower, and the skill of the finest craftsmen were all at the pharaoh's disposal. King Khufu must have been the most powerful pharaoh at that time, and his pyramid is the greatest. The decreasing size of the other two probably indicates the diminishing size of successive kings.

INCREDIBLE SCALE

The pyramids are the tallest buildings of the ancient world. In its original state, the Great Pyramid rose 481 feet (160 meters), and is estimated to have contained some 2,300,000 carefully shaped stone blocks, each weighing, on average, around two-and-a-half tons. It was the tallest building in the world until the nineteenth century. The Great Pyramid's vast size is hard to imagine today. It towers above famous landmarks in other countries, and the area it covered was large enough to hold the cathedrals of Florence, Milan, and St. Peter's in Rome, as well as St. Paul's and Westminster Abbey in London. Napoleon estimated that the blocks of stone from the three Giza pyramids would have been sufficient to build a wall of 10 feet (three meters) high and one foot (30 cm) thick around the whole of France, a claim which was verified by an eminent contemporary French mathematician.

THE GREAT SPHINX

Near the banks of the River Nile, the Great Sphinx seems to stand guard over the bodies of the great pharaohs. The Sphinx, a

Below: The pyramids of Giza – the Great Pyramid of Khufu (far left), and the pyramids of Khafre (center) and Menkaure (right).

Above: A nineteenth-century photograph of the Sphinx, which represents King Khafre with a lion's powerful body. In the background is his pyramid tomb.

Right: This pyramid, built by Pharaoh Khepren, is considered the "true," or perfect, architectural design for pyramids. The Sphinx, half human and half lion, lies on guard.

Taj Mahal, India   St. Peter's, Rome   Notre Dame, Paris

Step Pyramid, Saqqara   Great Pyramid (of Khufu), Giza   Pyramid of Khafre, Giza   Pyramid of Menkaure, Giza   Bent Pyramid, Dahshur

Above: The pyramids tower above famous landmarks in other countries.

Left: A nineteenth-century photograph showing tourists being helped to climb the stones of the Great Pyramid. The pyramid was robbed of its fine limestone outer casing over the years.

mythical creature with the body of a crouching lion and the head of a man – probably a portrait of King Khafre – was carved from a single rock of limestone protruding from the desert. Its paws are made out of stone blocks. This formidable creature stands 66 feet (20 meters) high, and about 240 feet (73 meters) long. The Sphinx originally represented the power of the pharaoh and of Egypt itself. In later generations, the Sphinx became the core of a cult of its own, and shrines were built around it.

CONSTRUCTING THE PYRAMID

Construction work on the pyramid started almost 4600 years ago. The millions of blocks of stone that make up the pyramid are of three main types from three sources. The great bulk of stone which forms the core is a poor quality limestone which occurs naturally in the near vicinity. Much finer white- limestone casing blocks which originally covered its entire surface were mined at Tura farther up the Nile.

The heaviest blocks, some weighing over 50 tons, used for lining the internal chambers and passages, are made of granite quarried at Aswan some 500 miles (800 km) away. Nearly all the quarries which supplied this stone were close to the banks of the Nile, so were the pyramids, which meant the river could be used to carry the stones by rafts. Each pyramid had a causeway connecting it to the Nile. This was a road cut out of the rocks which was eventually intended for the funeral procession. In the meantime, it formed a convenient road along which to drag the sledges carrying the stone to the pyramid.

There is no contemporary written evidence surviving that describes how the pyramids were built. The Greek historian Herodotus, who visited Egypt in the fifth century B.C., claimed that gangs of 100,000 workmen, rotating in shifts of three months each, toiled for 20 years building the Great Pyramid. Egyptologists now believe that it was built in less time by fewer men, however. Experts now believe that about 4000 laborers were employed to build the Great Pyramid. Considering the tools and equipment the Egyptians had to work with, that was remarkably quick.

PLANNING AND PRECISION

A great deal of survey and planning work would have been necessary before any building took place. Surviving sketches of other buildings suggest that the Egyptians would have made plans, and limestone models of different pyramids exist which may represent architectural planning aids. The site would need to be completely level before work commenced. They probably gauged this with accuracy by digging a trench of water around the square perimeter.

Geometrical precision was vital. The slightest error in the angle of incline of a pyramid would have resulted in a substantial misalignment of the edges at the apex. The principles of pyramid construction are familiar, but the exact procedure remains unknown. Therefore, some knowledge of mathematics,

Main picture:
Inside Pharaoh Khufu's pyramid.

1: Before burial, the "opening of the mouth" ceremony took place, which symbolically restored to the pharaoh his ability to speak.

2/3: The pharaoh was placed in a stone casket by priests, accompanied by mourners.

4: A burial chamber was cut out of the rock below the pyramid, but it was abandoned.

5: A second, higher up, was also abandoned.

6: The pharaoh was eventually buried in a third, even higher, chamber.

7: The chamber was filled with treasures, furniture, tools, weapons, and clothes, and finally the entrance was sealed.

geometry, and astronomy would also have been required for calculating the angles of the pyramid. The orientation of the Great Pyramid is incredibly accurate. The four sides, each measuring over 700 feet (230 meters) long, are aligned almost exactly on true north, south, east, and west.

ACCURACY

These alignments are so accurate that compass errors can be checked against them. This is an amazing achievement considering that the magnetic compass was unknown to the Ancient Egyptians. They probably managed to obtain such accuracy by observing a northern star rising and setting. The cardinal points, north and south, could have been established by taking measurements with a plumb line.

It is certain that the various courses of stone were laid from the center outward, since there are places where the central core blocks have been exposed beneath the casing blocks. It is also evident that they smoothed these final casing blocks from the top downward.

We do not know how the blocks were raised from ground level to their final position in the Great Pyramid. It is likely that massive supply and construction ramps were built round the building area. The heavy blocks would have been dragged up these ramps on sleds to the

Above right: Plan of the Giza pyramid complex.

Below right: Cross-section of the Great Pyramid of King Khufu.

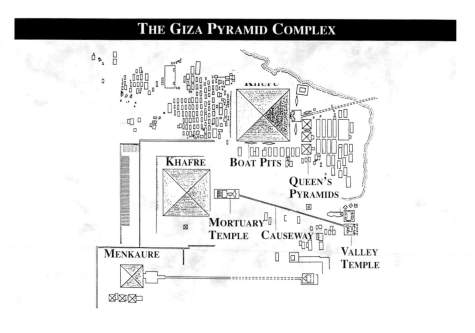

THE GIZA PYRAMID COMPLEX

KHUFU

KHAFRE   BOAT PITS

QUEEN'S PYRAMIDS

MORTUARY TEMPLE   CAUSEWAY

MENKAURE

VALLEY TEMPLE

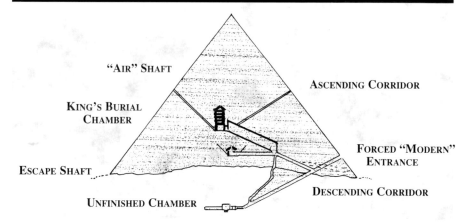

THE GREAT PYRAMID OF KING KHUFU

"AIR" SHAFT

ASCENDING CORRIDOR

KING'S BURIAL CHAMBER

FORCED "MODERN" ENTRANCE

ESCAPE SHAFT

DESCENDING CORRIDOR

UNFINISHED CHAMBER

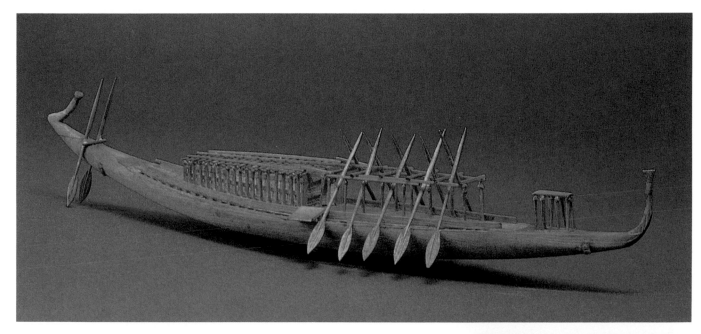

working platform. The remains of ramps have been discovered at the Maidum pyramid. They may also have used a kind of scaffolding for dressing it with limestone.

INSIDE THE PYRAMID

Throughout history, the huge mass of stone of the Great Pyramid has inspired people to believe that many secrets lie hidden within it. The early Christians believed the pyramids to be the granaries of Joseph, while generations of Arabs were convinced that they contained fantastic treasure. Despite various structural security measures, the burial treasure they did contain was looted when tomb-robbers broke in, probably before 2000 B.C.

The interior of the Great Pyramid consists of an approach passage and the burial chamber itself. When nineteenth-century archeol-

ogists entered the pyramid through the grand gallery, only the stone casket, which was larger than the doorway, remained intact. The slanted roof and cross-beams of granite in the burial chamber are to support the colossal weight above it.

The passage leading to it is wider at the top to enable the narrower entrance to be sealed with giant plug-blocks of granite. The design of the interior only appears complicated because the location of the burial chamber was changed twice during its construction. The two so-called "ventilation shafts" may have been a symbolic means of exit for the dead king's spirit. Later pyramid texts describe the king as mounting to heaven on the rays of the sun. The pyramid itself could have represented the rays of the sun shining down on Earth. Perhaps it was also conceived, as was the Babylonian

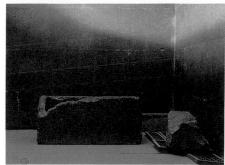

Top: A model of the funeral boat of King Khufu discovered in a pit near the Great Pyramid in 1951.

Above: When nineteenth-century archeologists entered the pyramid, they found that looters had stolen the body and treasures. Only the stone casket remained intact.

Right: Explorers in the ninteenth century investigate Khufu's tomb. Khufu's name in hieroglyphs appears in only one place in his pyramid. These explorers found it, above his burial chamber.

Below: A model funeral boat which would have carried the deceased on their final journey on the Nile to their tomb.

ziggurat, as a sort of stairway to heaven.

BURYING KHUFU

Pharaoh Khufu's pyramid was made ready for him before his death in 2,566 B.C. The site included subsidiary pyramids where the pharaoh's wives were to be buried, and masta-ba tombs – rectangular tombs intended for officials. A mortuary temple, reached via covered passageways, or causeways, was situated on one side. The causeways led from the valley temples to the mortuary temples alongside the pyramids. After Khufu's death, his body was taken by boat to the pyramid site and the boat was buried. This boat was

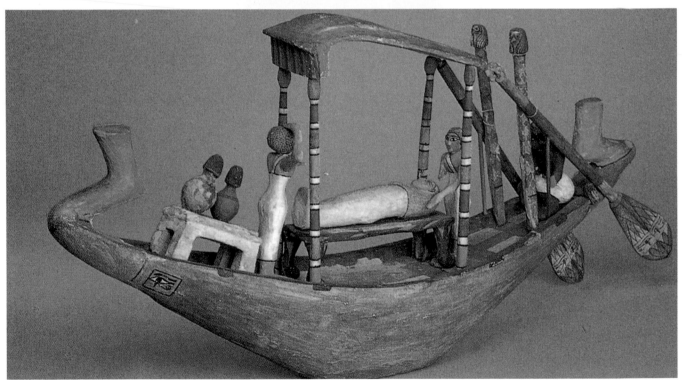

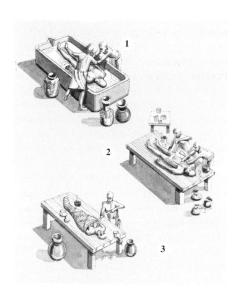

Above: (1) The body was preserved with strong salt, and the internal organs were removed. (2) Fragrant ointments were then rubbed in. (3) Finally, the body was wrapped in bandages.

rediscovered in a pit near the Great Pyramid in 1951. It had been carefully dismantled into its component parts after the king's funeral, but has now been reconstructed.

PREPARING THE BODY

The body was then mummified. First, it was preserved with strong salt, and the internal organs were removed. Fragrant ointments were then rubbed in, and finally the body was wrapped in bandages. Before burial, the "opening of the mouth" ceremony took place which symbolically restored to the pharaoh his ability to speak. A burial chamber was cut out of the rock below the pyramid, but it was abandoned. A second, higher, chamber was

also abandoned. The pharaoh was eventually buried in a third, even higher, chamber. He was placed in a stone casket by priests accompanied by mourners. The chamber was carefully filled with things that the pharaoh would need in the afterlife – food and drink, treasures, furniture, tools, weapons, and clothes, even models of servants and guards. Finally, the entrance was sealed.

A GREAT EXPLORER

The Italian-born explorer Giovanni Battista Belzoni was the first person in modern times to enter the pyramid of Khafre. To his dismay, the pharaoh's sarcophagus – casket – in his burial chamber was empty. Belzoni was born in 1778. Before traveling to Egypt in 1815 in search of ancient sites, he worked as a "strong man" in a theatrical act in England. From Egypt, he sent back many statues and other monuments to England. In 1921, his objects were displayed in an exhibition in London – which Belzoni himself attended. He died two years later in Africa, while searching for the source of the River Nile.

PYRAMIDS OF THE MIDDLE KINGDOM

The end of the Old Kingdom, when the pyramids at Giza were built, was followed by 150 years of civil war in Egypt. Eventually, order was restored and a new dynasty of pharaohs heralded the beginning of the Middle Kingdom, from 2040–1782 B.C. During this period, pyramids were again built by the pharaohs, but for the last time. The first notable pyramid was that of King Mentuhotep, who constructed it on the flat roof of his mortuary temple at Deir-el-Bahri on the west bank of the Nile opposite the ancient city of Thebes. Mentuhotep was the first pharaoh of the Middle Kingdom. He reigned for 50 years and restored

Below: King Mentuhotep was the first pharaoh of the Middle Kingdom. He ruled for 50 years. He was buried in a temple with a small pyramid structure on top.

order to the land of Egypt. He was buried in a temple with a small pyramid structure on top.

LOOTING THE PYRAMIDS

Rumors of the treasures hidden inside pyramids have fascinated people throughout history. By 1000 B.C., every known pyramid had been looted by thieves. The pyramids of Giza were the finest achievement of the Egyptian builders. Yet, despite the attempts made by their designers and builders to try and stop thieves from getting in, the burial chambers did not remain undisturbed for long. As a result, pyramid-building declined. and structures of this size would never be built again.

For a time, much smaller pyramids were built, in places such as Abusir. The interiors were constructed not of stone bricks but of mud-bricks and rubble – which meant that they soon crumbled away. Little effort, too, was made to conceal the entrances. However, a resurgence in pyramid-building occurred during the Middle Kingdom, between 2040–1782 B.C. Much more attention was paid to ways of keeping looters out, including false passages and trapdoors.

In the most elaborate of the Middle Kingdom pyramids – King Amenemhet III's pyramid at Hawara, southwest of Maidum – many attempts were made to fool the looters. This king was determined to defeat the tomb-

robbers who consistently found their way into these tombs and plundered the treasures they found there, and so he filled his pyramid with cunning devices. Architects went to enormous lengths to disguise the entry to the burial chamber. The entrance passage appeared to lead nowhere – but a stone in the roof slid across to give access to an upper corridor. This also appeared to lead nowhere, but a hidden brick door in the wall led to a third passage. Two further sliding roof blocks blocked the way to the burial chamber.

Nevertheless, thieves managed to enter and steal the treasures – perhaps the very people who sealed the pyramids later broke in again. The thieves who broke into Amenemhet III's pyramid dropped a lighted torch in the burial chamber – which destroyed everything. In the future, Egyptian kings would have to think of another way of preserving the sanctity of their tombs.

THE END OF PYRAMID-BUILDING

During the New Kingdom (1570-1070 B.C.), the pharaohs ceased to build pyramids as their tombs, realizing perhaps that no device, however complex, could stop determined thieves. Instead, less noticeable tombs, cut into hillsides, were preferred. The only intact king's burial chamber ever found belonged to King Tutankhamun, who was buried in a tomb in the Valley of the Kings, the famous burial site on the west bank of the Nile. Most of these graves were discovered and robbed hundreds of years ago, but Tutankhamun's grave lay undisturbed for almost 3000 years.

Left: The Valley of the Kings. Many pharaohs and their wives are buried here, in graves tunneled deep into the rocky hillside.

MUMMIES AND TOMBS

Why did the Egyptians go to so much expense and trouble to preserve their dead? They not only built vast pyramids to protect the tombs of important dead people, but they also went to enormous lengths to preserve the body inside the tomb. Important people often designed their own tombs while they were still alive. The reason why they went to such trouble is because they believed that the survival of the body was essential for the soul to become immortal. Life after death was thought to be a recreation of the best moments of Earthly existence, and so bodies were buried with their favorite possessions, a supply of food, and even model laborers to do their work for them. There was nothing morbid in this lifelong preoccupation with death – on the contrary, brightly painted mummy cases reflect an optimism and confidence in eternal life.

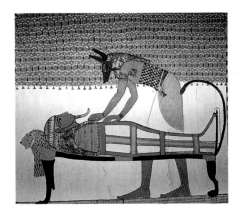

Above: In this tomb-painting, made around 1300 B.C., the jackal-headed god Anubis is shown bending over a mummified body. Anubis was believed to act as a guide to souls during their journey through the kingdom of the dead.

Previous page: Gilded mummy mask made from cartonnage, a material composed of linen or papyrus coated in plaster.

The precious objects put into a tomb alongside a dead person were chosen with great care. They included food and drink, models of servants and guards, and even means of travel: Egyptians believed that the souls of the dead were carried to the next world on funeral boats. This was because the purpose of an Egyptian burial was to help the dead person live again "for millions and millions of years." Life on Earth was uncertain and sometimes sad; true happiness was to be found after death. A tomb was, therefore, a "house of eternity." The Egyptians believed that by carefully preserving a dead body, you would also preserve its spirit, and give it everlasting life.

MUMMIES

Mummies are perhaps the most famous and intriguing type of evidence to have survived from Egyptian times. It is an extraordinary feeling to be able to look at the face – however crumbling or shriveled – of somebody who lived over 4000 years ago. But what exactly are they, and how and why were they made? Although the word "mummy" is associated with Ancient Egypt, it is also applied to preserved bodies from many other cultures. The word itself comes from the Arabic name

for bitumen, and was used to describe these bodies because their black appearance suggested that they had been coated in pitch. Most of the bandaged mummies that have survived date from the New Kingdom or the later half of Egyptian history. By this time, the embalming process, which had previously been reserved for royalty, became available to all who could afford it.

EXAMINING THE MUMMY

The outer casings of a mummy, and the casket or sarcophagus in which it was buried, can tell us a lot about the Egyptians' religious beliefs and, sometimes, about the long, complicated funeral ceremonies they arranged. We can discover how old mummified people were when they died, some of the illnesses they had suffered from, and, probably, how wealthy they had been. We may even be able to find out what individual Egyptians looked like, or how they wished to be remembered.

BELIEF IN THE AFTERLIFE

Ancient Egyptians' belief in an afterlife, and the development of embalming, are thought to have arisen partly in response to the survival of many naturally preserved bodies from the earliest times in Egypt. In this

Left: Wooden box with figures of workers.

Right: The face of Tutankhamun's mummy was covered with this funeral mask, made of pure gold, decorated with precious stones and colored glass.

Right: The earliest surviving mummy, from the tomb of Nefer at Saqqara, c. 2400 B.C.

predynastic period, the naked body was simply buried in a shallow grave in the desert. The hot, dry sand quickly absorbed the moisture from the body and prevented decay.

Some of these corpses must have been exposed by grave-robbers or shifting sands, and their discovery may have inspired later generations to believe in an afterlife. As time passed, this belief led to the need for a more dignified burial, which was accompanied by an increasing amount of provisions for the next life. The tomb replaced the simple grave, but this allowed the body to come into contact with the air and decompose. From the early sand burials, the Egyptians must have realized that the best way of preserving a body was to dehydrate it.

Making the mummies was a skilled and unpleasant process. Bodies rotted quickly in the hot sun. Dehydrating the body would prevent bacteria from breeding and causing decay. Many ordinary people could not afford a beautifully decorated mummy or casket, however: their bodies were preserved as quickly and cheaply as possible. In contrast, the families of important people lavished a great deal of money and time in preparing the best possible mummy for their dead relative.

PRESERVING THE BODY

Mummies were made by specialist workers, who became very skilled at their gruesome job. There was a ready supply of natural sodium salts to be found in Egypt, called natron, which are an effective drying agent and mildly antiseptic. With the aid of natron, the Ancient Egyptians developed an elaborate technique of embalming which could take as long as 70 days.

The first stage of this process was to

remove all the internal organs except the heart. This was left since it was thought to be the center of human intelligence which would be required for judgement in the underworld. The other organs were dried with natron and placed in four containers called canopic jars. Each was mixed with scented gum and sealed in a separate jar. Hawk-headed jars held intestines. The empty body was then washed with palm wine and spices and left to dry out, covered with natron salts, which dried and preserved it. Bodies were kept in natron for up to 60 days – the longer, the better. The dried body was packed with linen and spices to give it form again, then coated with molten resin to toughen it and make it waterproof.

BANDAGING THE MUMMY

The mummy was then bandaged with great care, since the tightness of the wrapping would help to keep the shape of the body. A mummy was recently unwrapped which was covered

Above: The body of a man preserved naturally by the hot, dry sand in which he was buried. The heat of the sand absorbed the moisture without which bacteria cannot breed and cause decay. Ironically. this humble form of burial preserved the body far better than the most elaborate tombs and costly embalming techniques. C. 3200 B.C. (British Museum.)

STOPPING THE ROT

Left: Even the inside of the sarcophagus was richly decorated with images of the gods from the under-world, for example, Osiris and Isis.

Right: (1) First the soft tissues – heart, lungs, stomach, brain, and intestines – were removed. (2) The body was packed with natron, a chemical which preserved it. (3) Then the body was smeared with ointments and herbs. (4) Finally, the body's limbs were arranged in a dignified way and tightly bound with bandages. Now it could be placed in its decorated casket and was ready for burial. Hopefully, it would last for ever.

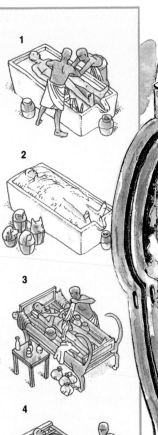

1

2

3

4

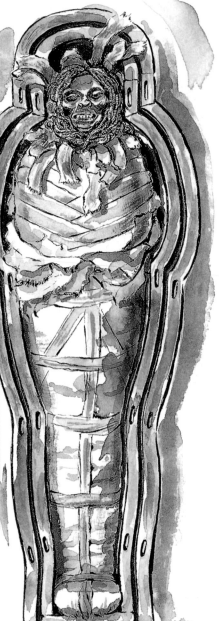

Above: Painted wooden casket and mummy of a Theban priestess, c. 1000 B.C. (British Museum.)

in a total of 3 miles (5 km) of three-inch- (7.5 cm) wide linen bandages. The wrappings usually bound the arms against the body and held the legs together. But there are some mummies whose limbs were separately wrapped.

Various protective amulets were distributed in the wrappings, usually in prescribed positions. An important amulet was the heart scarab, which was placed on the chest of the mummy. It was inscribed with a religious text instructing the person's heart not to make trouble for them when weighed in judgement before Osiris. Another popular protective amulet was the eye of Horus, or "udjat," which represented the eye of a falcon, with its characteristic markings beneath. Noble bodies also had face masks, often made from gold and precious stones. These were representations of what the dead person looked like.

A RICH BUSINESS

Most of the hundreds of mummies distributed throughout the world in museums and collections date from the late period, when entire families were buried together in communal catacombs. Richly painted religious scenes on these coffins replaced the need for individual tombs. From the time that mummies acquired a market value, these tombs, in which the mummies were stacked, were thoroughly ransacked by villagers living near the Theban cemeteries.

FAKE MUMMIES

In the sixteenth century, mummies were thought to have special healing properties, and many were ground up to make medicines. In order to meet the rising demand for this thriving business, fake mummies were produced using the corpses of executed criminals. In the last century, mummies were also ground

Above: Head of a male mummy with an inlaid eye, c. 1000 B.C.

Above: The Egyptians mummified many animals, such as this calf, c. 30 B.C.

up to be used as a brown artists' pigment and sold in tubes labeled "mummy." The Ancient Egyptians also mummified all manner of sacred animals, which were placed in a special sanctuaries beneath temples. Vast quantities of these have survived. At the turn of the century, some 300,000 cat mummies were shipped to Liverpool, to be turned into fertilizer and sold for £4 a ton.

The unwrapping and autopsy of mummies continues to be carried out in various institutions by leading medical specialists using the latest techniques and equipment. Powerful electron microscopes, forensic tests, and x-rays can often reveal the diseases that the Ancient Egyptians suffered from, the cause of their death, and their diet. Examination of the teeth of mummies can indicate what foods they ate, and there is even evidence that they practised dentistry. Some teeth have been found to contain a form of mineral cement, or have been bound together with fine gold wire. By detecting blood groups and hereditary traits from royal mummies, it is also possible to identify particular family connections. Establishing the age of certain kings at the time of death can also help specialists to verify the dates of various dynasties or important events in Egyptian history.

THE HOUSE OF THE SPIRIT

Although the basic function of the casket was to protect the body from violation by wild animals and thieves, it was also regarded as the house of the spirit. Through the magical powers of its decoration and inscriptions, it

Left: The god Osiris – king of the dead – protected by falcons, from a painted casket, c. 1050 B.C. (British Museum.)

Above: Gilded wooden inner casket of a Theban priestess, c. 1290 B.C.

Right: Wooden shabti figure of King Amenhotep III. These figures were placed in tombs to carry out agricultural work for the deceased in the afterlife.

could ensure the welfare of the deceased in the afterlife.

The casket underwent various changes in shape, material, and decoration throughout the long period of Ancient Egyptian history. Some of the earliest caskets were small and made of clay, basketwork or wood, where the body lay in a hunched-up position on its side. In the Middle Kingdom, full-length double wooden caskets were often provided. The inner one could be made in the shape of the mummy, while the outer was rectangular.

On the inside, this rectangular casket was decorated with personal objects and magical texts, while on the outside it had a large pair of eyes painted in a panel by the left shoulder so that the mummy inside could look out at the world. These eyes were often painted above a representation of a doorway, through which the mummy's spirit could leave at will and so have access to the rest of the tomb.

Mummies often had more than one casket: for example, Tutankhamun had four. They were made from wood which was then heavily decorated on the outside with paint and gold leaf. Even the inside of the sarcophagus was richly decorated with images of the gods from the underworld, such as Osiris and Isis. This was done so that the dead person might have a fair judgement from these gods.

ANIMAL MUMMIES

The Egyptians worshiped animals kept at certain temples, like the Apis bulls at Memphis, or the cats at Bubastis. To show their respect for the gods, they often turned these sacred animals into mummies when they died, and buried them close to the temple. They thought that this would win them favors from the gods. Some temples even bred animals

Above: Bronze figure of the sacred Apis bull (British Museum.)

specially for sacrifice and later mummification. Thousands of dead hawks have been found at the temple dedicated to the hawk-god Horus in fields near his temple at Edfu.

The Egyptians mummified dead people in the hope of providing them with everlasting life. While their bodies survived, their spirits would also. But in preserving their dead people as mummies, the Ancient Egyptians have also helped to keep alive the memory of their magnificent civilization for many thousands of years.

The characteristic caskets in the shape of the mummified body with an idealized face mask mostly date from the New Kingdom or later. The stereotyped faces often had a false beard to symbolize their identification with the dead king Osiris. The coffins were painted with a representation of the sky goddess, Nut, who spread her wings

Right: A finely carved wooden face from a casket, with inlaid eyes of lapis lazuli and glass.

protectively over the lid, since she was traditionally the mother of the deceased who was associated with her godly son, Osiris. The caskets were usually made of thin planks of wood skillfully doweled together, and the arms of the mummy were often shown carved in high relief and crossed over the chest. Painted bands of jewelry and floral collars reproduced the ornaments on the actual mummy. The head of the mummy was often enclosed in a mask

of cartonnage – layers of linen stuck together and covered with a thin coat of plaster. This mask was often extended to cover the complete body, and formed an ideal ground for elaborate decoration. Sometimes a painted and modeled board was placed over the body inside the casket as an economical way of suggesting a double coffin.

In the Saite period (after 600 B.C.), some superb hard-stone mummiform caskets were

Below: Scene showing the weighing of the mummy's heart as part of the judgement in the afterlife. From the Book of the Dead *of the scribe Hunefer, c. 1310 B.C.*

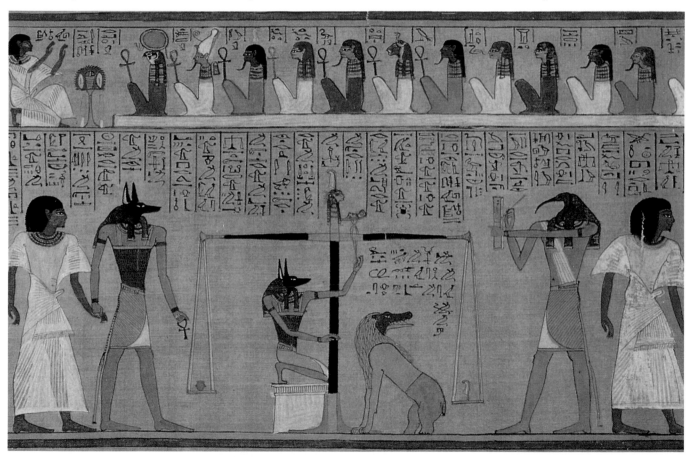

made, and the mummy was often covered in a bead net. By the late period, many corpses were not even properly embalmed, being simply painted with pitch and wrapped with bandages. Although the vital organs were often left in the body, "dummy" canopic jars were still provided for them which had a purely symbolic function. By Greco-Roman times, the idealized face mask was often placed with a more realistic portrait painted on a wooden panel, while the bandages were arranged in intricate geometric patterns.

Few royal caskets have survived, but the evidence is that they were of gilded wood, inlaid with stones and glass paste. Surviving intact examples are the three-nested caskets of Tutankhamun. They were enclosed in a rectangular stone sarcophagus decorated inside and out with funeral gods in painted relief.

One of the finest stone sarcophagi is that of King Seti I, which is of white calcite inlaid with rows of funerary figures in blue paste. The kings of the twenty-first and -second dynasties from Tanis (*c.* 950 B.C.) were buried in mummiform caskets of silver and gilded wood, two of them with silver hawks' heads.

TOMBS

The mummy's eternal dwelling place was the tomb. The type of tomb varied according to the period, the area, and the owner's social status. It is important to remember that the vast majority of poor Ancient Egyptians would have had a simple burial in the desert with few possessions. The tombs of the privileged who could afford more elaborate burial were either built of stone and brick or cut out of the solid rock. They all generally consist of two main parts: the burial chamber and the funerary chapel. The Old Kingdom tombs had a false door which served as a magical entrance through which the spirit of the deceased could pass from the burial chamber on the western side of the tomb into the chapel on the east. Here the spirit could partake of the offerings of food and drink provided by the relatives or priests.

In the carved reliefs on the walls of the tomb, scenes of farming, hunting, fishing, baking, and brewing ensured that provisions for the deceased would be continually available. As time went on, these were supplemented by representational models and a large variety of personal possessions. The royal tombs in the Valley of the Kings at Thebes were completely closed, with entrance stairs to four passages or corridors, a hall, and a burial chamber. These all had a symbolic significance in the journey of the spirit in the afterlife.

This journey of the spirit is recorded in

Below: Tomb of Queen Nefertiti, wife of Ramses II. It is probably the most beautifully painted Ancient Egyptian tomb, c. 1240 B.C.

detail on papyri, which were often placed in tombs from the New Kingdom onward. These religious writings are known as *Books of the Dead,* and were copies of earlier Old Kingdom stone inscriptions called the pyramid texts.

The principal magical function of these writings was to secure for the deceased a satisfactory afterlife, and to give him the power to leave his tomb when necessary. They include painted depictions of Anubis, the god

Above: Papyrus with a hymn to the god Ra from the Book of the Dead. *Hieroglyphs came to used almost exclusively for religious and magical texts. C. 1050 B.C.*

of mummification, and show the final judgement before Osiris, the king of the dead. The mummy's personality or spirit is identified with the Ba bird, which is portrayed as a human-headed bird hovering over the mummy.

ROYAL TOMBS

The royal tombs in the valleys of the Kings and Queens at Thebes were looted continuously in ancient times. In order to prevent further violation, the mummies were removed secretly by the Theban priests, and most of them were hidden in a deep shaft in the cliff face. Although they were eventually discovered by villagers in the last century, who began to profit from the discovery, they were rescued by the Egyptian Antiquities Service. When they were transported to Cairo for the museum in 1881, the customs officer at the city gates levied a duty on them, classifying them as dried fish!

Right: Wooden jackal, sacred to the god Anubis. These figures were placed in tombs symbolically to guard the dead. (British Museum.)

TUTANKHAMUN'S TOMB

It was in the Valley of the Kings that one of the most important and revealing tombs was discovered: that of Pharaoh Tutankhamun. This discovery was one of the most exciting events in twentieth-century archeology. Explorers knew that many rulers of Ancient Egypt had been buried in the Valley of the Kings, but they also knew that most of these graves had been robbed long ago. Tutankhamun's tomb had itself been disturbed at some time in the past – but the robbers had failed to discover the secret burial chamber where the mummified body of the young pharaoh lay hidden. For 35 centuries, knowledge of Tutankhamun's grave was hidden.

During the nineteenth and early twentieth centuries, many explorers traveled to Egypt, hoping to

discover more about its past. Howard Carter, the British archeologist who discovered Tutankhamun's tomb in 1922, spent many years of his life studying the remains of Ancient Egypt. Even with his expert knowledge, he was still amazed at the richness and beauty of the objects he found in Tutankhamun's tomb chambers. The array of valuable objects buried with the pharaoh shows how much more magnificent the tomb treasures of pharaohs greater than Tutankhamun must have been. For although he is now the most famous pharaoh in history, in his own time he was a fairly unimportant king who came to the throne when he was just nine years old.

A THRILLING DISCOVERY

An extract from a newspaper report of the discovery, published in 1922, records the thrill of the discovery: "Cautiously, the explorers edged their way along the narrow passage. They had no idea what lay ahead. They had already passed one sealed door. Now they came to another. Using a heavy iron spike, Carter cut a small hole at eye-level, so he could see (by flickering candlelight) into the next chamber. Eagerly, he peered into the gloomy darkness. Then he turned to Lord Carnarvon, his voice shaking with excitement: 'I see wonderful things...' he said." Later, Carter remembered that day – November 25, 1922 – as "the most wonderful I have ever lived through."

Lord Carnarvon, the wealthy patron who financed Carter's explorations, died suddenly and unexpectedly not long after Tutankhamun's tomb was discovered. People said that he had died as a result of "the Mummy's Curse" – the dead pharaoh's revenge on anyone who dared to disturb his tomb. In fact, Carnarvon died from infection

following a mosquito bite. But recently, scientists have suggested that disease-causing fungi may lurk in the ancient tombs, although we do not know for certain that they caused Carnarvon's death.

Tutankhamun's burial chamber reveals the immense wealth of the ruling royal family who prepared his tomb. His grave is probably the most famous and best-preserved of all Egyptian royal burials. Yet, despite its splendor and lavishness, it may not have been unique. The types of objects found there are typical of royal and noble status in this world, but also were designed to help him in the world of the dead.

THE TOMB

A plan of the tomb shows four separate chambers. Each chamber had a ritual purpose: the east room was for rebirth; the south for eternal royalty; the west for departure toward the funeral destinies, and the north for

Above: Lord Carnarvon, the wealthy patron who paid for Carter's explorations.

Left: Howard Carter and his team of archeologists in the Valley of the Kings. He spent many years investigating the ancient civilization of Egypt.

reconstitution of the body. These chambers are each filled with objects designed to be taken by the dead pharaoh to the afterlife. These included gilded wooden beds; a trumpet; gilded chariots; gaming boards inlaid with gold and ivory; pendants and bracelets set with gemstones; and a variety of statues.

Inside the burial chamber was a large box-like shrine that filled the entire room. Within it there were three more shrines. In the last of these was the king's sarcophagus, which held three caskets, each nesting one inside the other. The last casket held the mummified body of Tutankhamun. The two lifesize guardian figures inside the tomb are made of wood,

varnished black, with the pharaoh's features, and gilded. The face of Tutankhamun's mummy was covered with a funeral mask made of pure gold, decorated with precious stones and colored glass. The goddess Hathor, in the shape of a mother cow, watched over the body of the dead king. She wore the sun disk between her horns. The pharaoh's casket was decorated with pictures of the gods and goddesses who, the Egyptians hoped, would protect the young King Tutankhamun's soul in the world of the dead.

A NEW LIFE
Unlike many important people at this time,

Tutankhamun did not design his own tomb while he was still alive. This is probably because he died so young. It was left to royal officials to provide everything his spirit might need for its everlasting life, from food and drink to musical instruments and fans. But this new life was not to be lived in the tomb itself. That was simply where the body was kept. Tutankhamun's spirit, like everyone else's, had to travel to another world – the peaceful kingdom of the dead.

Far left: The face of one of two lifesize guardians of Tutankhamun's tomb. He is made of wood, varnished black, with his features and clothing gilded.

Left: Decoration from one of Tutankhamun's casket. It shows the gods and goddesses who, the Egyptians hoped, would protect the pharaoh's soul in the world of the dead.

Pyramids around the World

The shining example of the Egyptians inspired other civilizations to adopt the pyramid as a method of construction. From the Ancient Maya and Aztec people of South America, to the architects of the twentieth century, subsequent generations have mirrored Egypt's great pyramids in their buildings and monuments.

Above: For hundreds of years the Egyptians raided parts of Nubia, which was rich in gold and other natural resources. In this tomb-painting, Nubians bring gifts of precious stones and leopard skins to Pharoah Thutmose IV.

NUBIAN PYRAMIDS

Pyramids ceased to be built in Egypt during the New Kingdom (1570–1070 B.C.). Yet they rose again, some 350 years after the period had ended, in Nubia, the land that bordered southern Egypt and is today known as Sudan. During the eighth century B.C., a Nubian king called Piyi marched north and conquered Egypt to became the first pharaoh of the twenty-fifth dynasty (747–656 B.C.). Piyi and his successors were strongly influenced by Egyptian culture. They built pyramid tombs near their Nubian capital of Napata. Unlike the Egyptian pyramids, these were smaller at the base, with taller, steeper sides. They were built of stone, and their rulers were buried beneath them.

The last pharaoh of the dynasty, Tanutamun, was defeated by the Assyrians, who forced the Nubians out of Egypt. Tanutamun returned to Napata – which remained the capital of Nubia for the next 350 years.

Then, in about 300 B.C., the city of Meroë, which lay on the Nile south of Napata, became the royal capital. Here, for more than 600 years, Nubian kings continued to build their distinctive pyramids, nearly 50 of which have been discovered. For hundreds of years, the Egyptians raided parts of Nubia, which was rich in gold and other natural resources. The Nubians were influenced by the culture and religion of the Egyptians, their neighbors to the north.

Nubian rulers and nobles were buried in chambers carved out beneath pyramids that rose more steeply than the Egyptian ones. Each pyramid had a small chapel on its eastern side, built in the shape of an Egyptian temple. Inside the chapel stood a table on which the priests' offerings of food and drink for the dead person were placed. Stelae – free-standing upright stones inscribed with words from ritual texts – stood on each side. Here, priests said prayers. Carved stone figures called shabtis were placed in the tomb to act as a workforce for the dead king in the afterlife. Sometimes, though, servants were put to death and buried in the tomb so that they could serve their master or mistress in the next world.

THE ZIGGURATS OF SUMER

Rising like small mountains from the cities of Ancient Mesopotamia, ziggurats were large stepped structures made of mud-bricks.

Unlike the pyramids of Egypt, which were royal tombs, ziggurats had a purely religious function. On their summits stood a temple in which sacred rituals were performed to promote the prosperity of the city. Mesopotamia – now modern Iraq – lay between the Tigris and Euphrates rivers, and saw the rise of the world's first cities between about 4000 and 3000 B.C. The Sumerian people of this region used water from the two rivers to irrigate the land and grow crops. In time, small communities grew into cities, with strong walls, temples, and ziggurats.

The first large ziggurats appeared in southern Mesopotamia at the cities of Ur, Urduk, and Eridu during the reign of Ur-Nammu, king of Ur (2112-2095 B.C.). Three-storied ziggurats, such as the ziggurat of Ur, were common. But the later Assyrian ziggurat at Khorsabad in northern Mesopotamia had seven stories, each one painted a different color.

THE TOWER OF BABYLON

Rising more than 200 feet (61 meters) high above the ground, the ziggurat of Babylon was one of the marvels of the ancient world. Babylon was situated on the River Euphrates in southern Mesopotamia. The city first became important in the eighteeth century B.C. under King Hammurabi. During his reign, the ziggurat was first built.

One thousand years later, the ziggurat was rebuilt by King Nebuchadnezzar – Babylon's most important king. The rebuilt ziggurat was made of sun-dried mud-bricks and bitumen – waterproof tar. Inside the temple stood a golden table and couch on which the most important Babylonian god, Marduk, was said to rest. Babylon's ziggurat probably inspired the biblical story of the Tower of Babel – Babylon – which was intended to reach from Earth to heaven. In the biblical story, God prevented its completion by making its builders speak different languages and scattering them over the world.

CITY WALLS

Nebuchadnezzar also had splendid new temples, palaces, and gateways constructed. The city's inner wall was 90 feet (27 meters) high, with towers along its length. There was also an outer wall that surrounded the city. It may have been up to 10 miles (16 km) long. The walls were so wide that, according to the reports of the Greek historian Herodotus, a chariot with a team of four horses could be driven along them.

Above: This ceremonial helmet belonged to one of the kings of Ur. Cloth padding was found still inside it.

Left: The ziggurat at Babylon probably inspired the biblical story of the Tower of Babel (Babylon), which was intended to reach from Earth to heaven. This painting is by the northern European artist Peter Brueghel the Elder (1525-69).

A GLORIOUS GARDEN

Nebuchadnezzar also created a "hanging garden" for his foreign wife, who longed to be reminded of the gardens of her homeland. The gardens were considered one of the seven wonders of the ancient world. High stone terraces were covered with soil in which a great variety of trees and shrubs were planted. Staircases led up to the top terraces, and ingenious devices raised water up from the Euphrates to irrigate the trees.

Nebuchadnezzar conquered many nations and, according to legend, went mad for seven years because of his evil ways. During this time, he lived like an animal and ate grass.

PYRAMIDS OF THE AMERICAS

Pyramids were built not only in Egypt and Mesopotamia: impressive remains are also found throughout the Americas. During the nineteenth century, explorers discovered huge stepped pyramids. Many of them were crumbling in the harsh, mountainous lands of Central America.

On the flat summits stood temples which were used many centuries before in religious rituals, some of them involving grisly human sacrifices. These impressive stone structures had been built by Ancient American peoples, including the Teotihuacan people, the Maya, and the Aztecs.

THE MAYA AND THE AZTECS

The Maya had one of the most sophisticated cultures in the Ancient Americas. They were skilled in mathematics, and were the only Ancient American people to use writing widely. They were also fascinated by astronomy, and built great observatories in order to study the stars. Quite suddenly, however, their cities were abandoned in the ninth century A.D.

The Teotihuacan people lived at the same time as the Mayas, but they too vanished, leaving no written records. However, they left behind them the remains of a huge city – Teotihuacan – whose giant pyramids rivaled the pyramids of Giza in size.

The Aztecs emerged 500 years later. Their civilization built on the achievements of the Maya in such diverse fields as building, irrigation, astronomy, mathematics, weaving, and the arts.

Pyramidlike structures were also built in North America. They are known as mounds because they were made of earth. These structures were used as temples and palaces.

PALENQUE

The Maya built great cities such as Palenque and Tikal in a huge area that includes much of what is now Mexico, Guatemala, and Honduras.

Many of these cities, with their huge stone pyramids, temples, and palaces, lay hidden in thick jungle for over 900 years, since they were inexplicably abandoned by the Maya in about A.D. 900. Tikal, for example, the largest Mayan city, was only rediscovered by chance in 1848. Palenque, too, was only brought to public attention in the nineteenth century. Experts believe many more may still be undiscovered. Palenque lies in eastern Mexico at the edge of a rainforest. It flourished during the seventh century A.D., especially during the reign of a ruler named Lord Pacal. The city was adorned with palaces and temple-palaces, and a tower-like observatory from which Mayan astronomers studied the night skies.

In 1952, a Mexican archeologist was studying the Temple of the Inscriptions at Palenque, when he discovered a hidden entrance in the floor that led to a long stairway. When he had

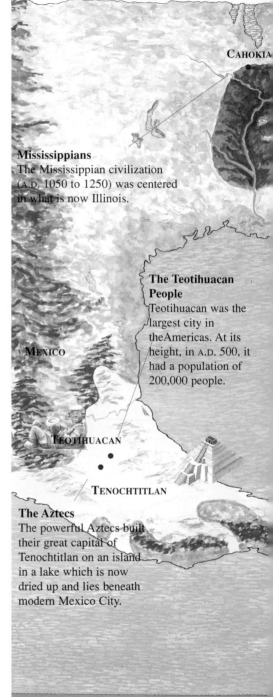

Mississippians
The Mississippian civilization (A.D. 1050 to 1250) was centered in what is now Illinois.

CAHOKIA

The Teotihuacan People
Teotihuacan was the largest city in the Americas. At its height, in A.D. 500, it had a population of 200,000 people.

MEXICO

TEOTIHUACAN

TENOCHTITLAN

The Aztecs
The powerful Aztecs built their great capital of Tenochtitlan on an island in a lake which is now dried up and lies beneath modern Mexico City.

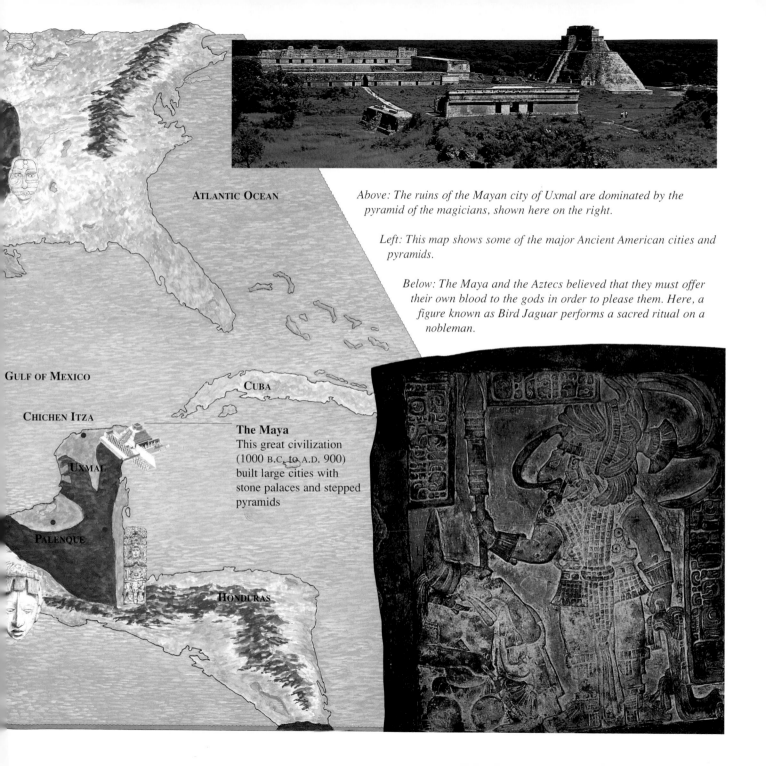

Above: The ruins of the Mayan city of Uxmal are dominated by the pyramid of the magicians, shown here on the right.

Left: This map shows some of the major Ancient American cities and pyramids.

Below: The Maya and the Aztecs believed that they must offer their own blood to the gods in order to please them. Here, a figure known as Bird Jaguar performs a sacred ritual on a nobleman.

ATLANTIC OCEAN

GULF OF MEXICO

CUBA

CHICHEN ITZA

UXMAL

PALENQUE

HONDURAS

The Maya
This great civilization (1000 B.C. to A.D. 900) built large cities with stone palaces and stepped pyramids

Right: The most magnificent building in Palenque was the Temple of the Inscriptions, an imposing, pyramid-temple over 80 feet (20 meters) high.

Below right: Many of the buildings at Teotihuacan were decorated with paintings of gods, as well as of animals such as serpents, coyotes, and jaguars. This wall-painting shows the rain god Tlaloc wearing a feather headdress, with water flowing from his hands.

Below: many of Teotihuacan's buildings remain standing today. This view shows the Avenue of the Dead from the Plaza of the Moon, with the Pyramid of the Sun on the left.

cleared away the debris, he made his way down to a tomb that had lain hidden for 1000 years. Inside was a decorated stone sarcophagus that held the body of Lord Pacal. A magnificent jade mask covered the king's face.

The Maya built their pyramids without the use of metal tools, pack animals, or the wheel. Once a site had been chosen, four stone walls were built. They were packed with stones and then plastered over so that the next stage could be built on top. As the pyramid rose, its walls were covered with limestone and creamy plaster, and parts of it were painted bright red.

THE CITY OF TEOTIHUACAN

The greatest pyramid ever built in the Ancient Americas was raised in the city of Teotihuacan, near what is now Mexico City. Here, the Pyramid of the Sun towered up in five chunky terraces. The area at its base almost rivaled that of the Great Pyramid of Giza. In fact, until the twentieth century, this pyramid was one of the largest structures in the Americas.

The buildings at the site were laid out on a grid system like a modern American city. Most people lived in one-storey apartment complexes that stretched out on each side of the Avenue of the Dead. Little is known about the people who lived in them, however. They left no written evidence, so scientists have had to study the remains of buildings, wall-paintings, and pottery for information.

AT ITS PEAK

Teotihuacan reached the peak of its influence around A.D. 500, when its population of 200,000 made it the largest city in the Americas. It was also an important religious center. The Aztecs, who became the dominant people in the area centuries later, regarded the city as the "place of the gods." They also buried

Above: The stone heads of Quetzalcoatl, the feathered serpent, and Tlaloc, appear on the Temple of Quetzalcoatl.

Left: This mosaic mask, made from 200 pieces of jade, covered the face of the Mayan king, Lord Pacal.

their rulers there. The fortunes of Teotihuacan began to decline in about A.D. 650. Then, 100 years later, a fire – perhaps caused by civil unrest – reduced the once-great city to a smoking ruin.

One of the most important religious buildings in Teotihuacan was the temple of the god Quetzalcoatl, situated at the southern end of the city. The temple's outer wall is carved with heads of Quetzalcoatl and the round-eyed rain god Tlaloc.

Quetzalcoatl, the feathered serpent, was often depicted with the body of a snake and the feathers of a bird, known as a quetzal. In Teotihuacan he was worshiped as a god of nature. But he was also revered by other Mexican civilizations. The Aztecs, for example, regarded him as the god of learning.

THE GREAT PYRAMID OF THE AZTECS

The Aztecs were a warlike people who controlled a vast empire from their capital, Tenochtitlan. In the early fourteenth century, the Aztecs settled in the Valley of Mexico.

Burial found under a triangular-shaped mound

Preparing Food
Animals such as deer caught by the Cahokians were hung on wooden frames, where they were skinned and prepared for cooking.

Types of Mound
Some of the mounds at Cahokia were long and triangular, others rounded, like cones. Some resembled pyramids with flat tops, on which temples were built.

Wooden Houses
Cahokia's houses were made of wooden poles and thatched with long prairie grass.

Monks' Mound
This vast earthen mound was built and rebuilt over 300 years ago. It was given the name "Monks' Mound" because it was inhabited by French monks in 1809.

From this time on, they grew more powerful and, by the end of the fifteenth century, their mighty empire numbered 10 million people.

THE GREAT TEMPLE
The Aztecs founded their capital city on a small island near the edge of Lake Texacoco. By 1500, Tenochtitlan had a population of about 100,000, and boasted impressive stone buildings. At the heart of the city was the grand ceremonial center. Inside, among pyramids, temples, and a ball-game court, a huge pyramid known as the Great Temple rose up some 98 feet (30 meters) high. Constructed around at least four older buildings, the Great Temple had a huge double staircase. Two temples, one dedicated to Tlaloc, the god of rain, the other to Huitzilopochtli, the god of the sun, rose up from the summit.

Here, on the summit, Aztec priests performed human sacrifices in the belief that the blood would give strength to their gods. Sometimes victims were skinned in honor of the god of springtime. Priests wore this skin to symbolize the rebirth of spring. When the Spanish invaded the Americas in the sixteenth century, their armies defeated the Aztec Empire, and Tenochtitlan was razed to the ground.

Left: The mysterious mound-builders. Large pyramidlike mounds of earth have been discovered in southern Illinois at Cahokia.

THE MYSTERIOUS MOUND-BUILDERS

Although stone pyramids were not built in North America, large pyramidlike mounds of earth have been discovered. The greatest of these lies in southern Illinois at Cahokia, the main city of a people known as the Mississippians. Little is known about them, because they did not have written records or stone monuments. However, they probably flourished from the eleventh to the thirteenth century A.D.

The city was enclosed by a 20-foot- (6-meter-) high fence made of wooden stakes that formed the shape of a capital "D." Guards were positioned along this fence. Inside the fence, Cahokia was dominated by a 100-foot- (30-meter-) high mound called "Monks' Mound." It gained this name because it was inhabited by French monks in 1809. On the highest of four terraces stood a tall building with a

Below: Aztec priests placed the hearts of sacrifice victims on stone human figures known as chac-mools.

Right: Aztec sacrificial knife.

Priest School

All Aztec boys went to school from the age of about 10 or 12. The sons, and sometimes the daughters, of wealthy people were sent to a calmerac, or religious school.

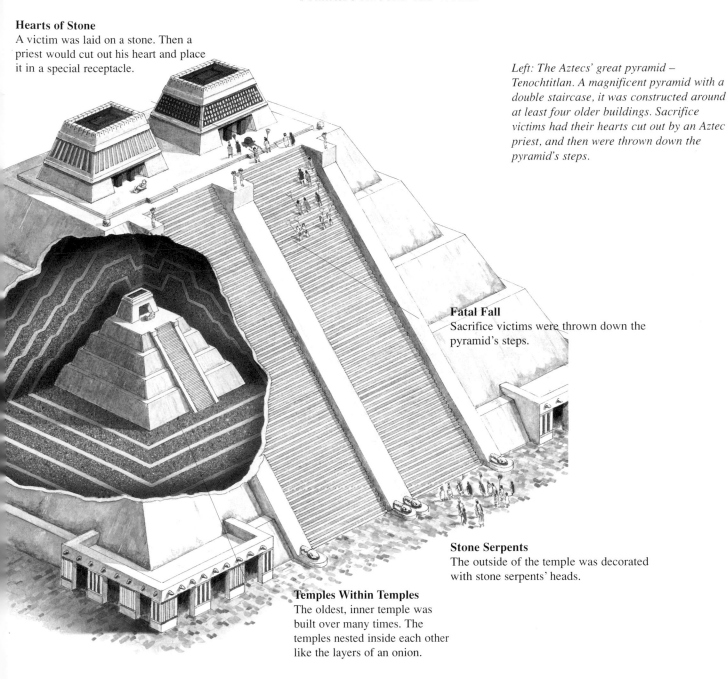

Hearts of Stone
A victim was laid on a stone. Then a priest would cut out his heart and place it in a special receptacle.

Left: The Aztecs' great pyramid – Tenochtitlan. A magnificent pyramid with a double staircase, it was constructed around at least four older buildings. Sacrifice victims had their hearts cut out by an Aztec priest, and then were thrown down the pyramid's steps.

Fatal Fall
Sacrifice victims were thrown down the pyramid's steps.

Stone Serpents
The outside of the temple was decorated with stone serpents' heads.

Temples Within Temples
The oldest, inner temple was built over many times. The temples nested inside each other like the layers of an onion.

thatched roof. This structure was probably used both as a temple and a residence for the Mississippian ruler.

Within Cahokia's perimeter fence were more than 100 smaller mounds of different shapes. Scholars believe that the chief ruler was also a priest, and may have been seen as the servant of the sun. In the late thirteenth century, Cahokia began to decline. The reasons are not known. It may have been due to a famine, warfare, or harsh climate conditions. But by the late 1400s, the city was abandoned.

Below left: Found on a strip of copper, this man's head, with its spiky hair and bared teeth, is thought to represent a Mississippian warrior.

Below right: A spider looks out from this shell disk, one of the objects found at Cahokia. The Cahokians used the shells of mussels and clams taken from rivers to make ornaments and objects such as spoons.

PYRAMIDS WORLDWIDE

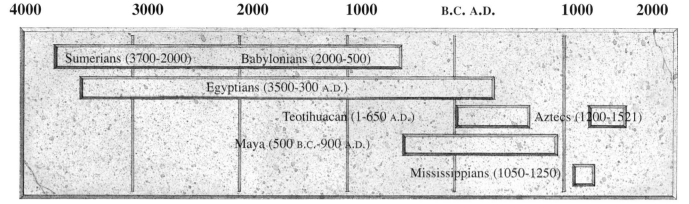

| 4000 | 3000 | 2000 | 1000 | B.C. A.D. | 1000 | 2000 |

Sumerians (3700-2000)   Babylonians (2000-500)

Egyptians (3500-300 A.D.)

Teotihuacan (1-650 A.D.)   Aztecs (1200-1521)

Maya (500 B.C.-900 A.D.)

Mississippians (1050-1250)

Pyramids did not die out with the end of the Ancient world. Pyramid-shaped structures, both ancient and modern, are found in many parts of the world. Some of the most important ones are listed here.

ABUSIR, EGYPT
The crumbling mounds of three pyramids, built by kings Sahure, Neferikare, and Niuserre, rise from the desert at Abusir, west of the Nile. Although they are small in comparison with the Giza pyramids, these buildings include the ruins of some impressive valley and mortuary temples.

BABYLON, IRAQ
The remains of this ancient city, with its huge ziggurat and legendary "hanging gardens," lie near Baghdad, the capital of Iraq. Babylon first became powerful in the eighteenth century B.C. But it was only under Nebuchadnezzar II in the sixth century B.C. that it became famous for its size and beauty.

CAHOKIA, U.S.A.
Situated in Illinois, Cahokia was founded in about A.D. 600. It is the largest ancient city in North America. More than 100 mounds, all

Below: The ziggurat was a stepped, pyramidlike structure built by the people of Ancient Mesopotamia. This is the remains of one at Ur, in Ancient Sumer.

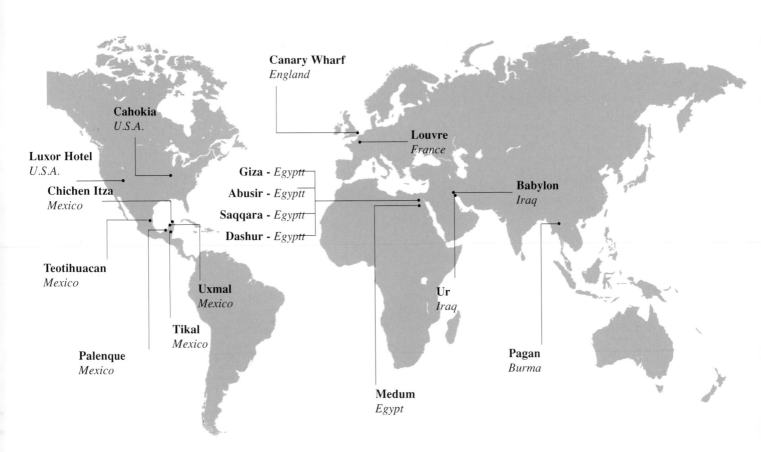

Canary Wharf
England

Cahokia
U.S.A.

Louvre
France

Luxor Hotel
U.S.A.

Chichen Itza
Mexico

Giza - *Egyptt*

Abusir - *Egyptt*

Babylon
Iraq

Saqqara - *Egyptt*

Dashur - *Egyptt*

Teotihuacan
Mexico

Uxmal
Mexico

Ur
Iraq

Tikal
Mexico

Palenque
Mexico

Pagan
Burma

Medum
Egypt

*Egypt is not the only place in the world
where pyramids are found. They were also
built in the Americas and elsewhere, as
shown in this map.*

made of earth, have been identified. The greatest of these is Monks' Mound, which contains more than 20 million cubic feet (600,000 cubic meters) of earth that was brought to the site in baskets.

CANARY WHARF, U.K.

This giant office building, built in the 1980s, rises over the River Thames in the east end of London. The roof of this 50-storey structure is topped by a pyramid. The machinery used to operate the lifts and air-conditioning is stored inside it.

CHICHEN ITZA, MEXICO

This city lies in the Yucatan Peninsula, and is one of Mexico's best-preserved sites. The structures, which show the influence of both Mayan and Toltec building styles, include several pyramids. Most impressive is the Castillo, which rises 76 feet (24 meters) high.

DAHSHUR, EGYPT

The bent pyramid of King Sneferu has made this site famous. The building is unique, not only for its shape, but also because it has not one, but two, entrances. Also at Dahshur is the Red Pyramid – so called for its reddish limestone – another spectacular construction built by Sneferu.

LOUVRE, FRANCE

One of the wonders of the modern world, this glass pyramid was built at the entrance to the Louvre Museum in Paris. Opened in 1989 by President Mitterand, the structure is made of a frame of steel girders. The pyramid is used as a visitors' reception to the museum.

LUXOR HOTEL, U.S.A.

This grand hotel, situated in Las Vegas, was built in the shape of a pyramid and opened in 1993. The building rises 30 stories high, and has some 5000 rooms. Its exterior consists of black reflecting glass. A replica of the Great Sphinx keeps guard outside.

MAIDUM, EGYPT

The towerlike core of the pyramid at Maidum represents the remains of the first true pyramid built by the Egyptians. The structure collapsed some time after it was completed more than 4500 years ago. To the north and south of the pyramid lie cemeteries full of brick mastaba tombs.

PAGAN, BURMA

The remains of this ancient city lie next to the Irrawaddy River. Many of the buildings are about 1000 years old, and were erected by a succession of Burmese kings. They include an array of Buddhist temples that rise up in terraces like stepped pyramids.

Left: The three largest pyramids of Giza in Egypt are the greatest stone monuments to have survived from ancient times.

PALENQUE, MEXICO
Situated in the lowlands of eastern Mexico, this Mayan city flourished in the seventh century A.D. The site includes a palace and five temples. The most impressive of these is the Temple of the Inscriptions, in which was found the tomb of a ruler named Lord Pacal.

SAQQARA, EGYPT
This site is known for the impressive step pyramid built for King Djoser. But 14 other pyramids have also been located – most of them now piles of rubble – and more seem likely to be unearthed.

TEOTIHUACAN, MEXICO
The largest and most impressive site in Mexico, this vast city boasts the greatest pyramid in the Ancient Americas: the Pyramid of the Sun.

TIKAL, GUATEMALA
The pale stone structures of this Mayan city rise from the Guatemalan jungle. The site covers 6 square miles (16 square km) and is dominated by soaring pyramids, in particular the nine-terraced Temple of the Giant Jaguar.

UR, IRAQ
The ziggurat of Ur was built around a core of mud-bricks during the reign of Ur-Nammu, about 4000 years ago. The site is one of the great cities of the Sumerian people of southern Mesopotamia.

UXMAL, MEXICO
This Mayan city lies on the Yucatan Peninsula in eastern Mexico. It flourished during the second half of the first millennium A.D. Its structures include the Pyramid of the Old Women, and the magnificent Pyramid of the Magician.

Right: The dramatic pyramid that stands at the Louvre Museum, Paris. It was opened in 1989.